Nature's Children

OLD WORLD
MONKEYS

Bill Ivy

GROLIER
EDUCATIONAL

FACTS IN BRIEF

Classification of Old World Monkeys — 182 6776

Class: *Mammalia* (mammals)
Order: *Primates* (monkeys, apes, lemurs, people)
Family: *Cercopithecidae*
Subfamilies: *Cercopithecinae* (monkeys with cheek pouches)
Colobinae (leaf monkeys)
Genus: There are 12 genera of Old World Monkeys.
Species: There are over 70 species of Old World Monkeys.

World distribution. Africa, India, China, Japan and Southeast Asia.

Habitat. Varies with species.

Distinctive physical characteristics. Most species have arms and legs of equal length, opposable thumbs and big toes, and a long tail. The nostrils are curved, close together and open downwards. There are thick calluses on the buttocks.

Habits. Live in communities of 4 to 100. Most sleep in trees at night. Mainly active during the day.

Diet. Varies with species.

Published originally as
"Getting to Know ... Nature's Children."

This series is approved and recommended by the Federation of Ontario Naturalists.

This library reinforced edition is available exclusively from:

GROLIER
EDUCATIONAL
Sherman Turnpike, Danbury, Connecticut 06816

Contents

Which animals do you think are the most popular ones at the zoo? Probably the monkeys and for good reason. With their expressive faces and humorous antics they often remind us of mischievous little people. In fact, when people play pranks we may say they are up to "monkey business" and when we are teased by our friends we may tell them to stop "monkeying around."

Monkeys are not only playful, they are curious, noisy, intelligent and they're great acrobats as well. People have always been fascinated by them and in some countries monkeys are considered sacred.

Want to have more fun than a barrel of monkeys? Then turn the page and learn more about these incredible animals.

Barbary macaque.

Old or New

Most monkeys live in the tropics where the weather is always warm but a few live in areas where the winters are very cold. Scientists divide monkeys into two groups. Those that live in Central and South America are called New World monkeys, while those found in Africa and Asia are called Old World monkeys.

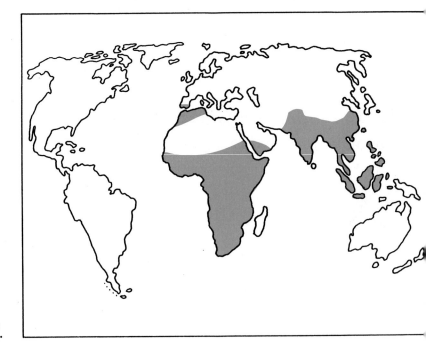

The shaded areas on this map show where Old World monkeys are found.

There are several ways to tell which group a particular monkey belongs to even if you don't know where it came from. If the monkey has a prehensile, or grasping, tail and can use it as an extra hand for picking up things or swinging from trees, it is a New World monkey. No Old World monkey can do these things with its tail. You can also tell by looking closely at the monkey's face. Old World monkeys have nostrils that are close together and open towards the front. The nostrils of a New World monkey are wide, round, and further apart, and they open to the sides.

Only Old World monkeys have their own handy seat cushions, pads of tough skin on their bottom to make sitting more comfortable. Some also have cheek pouches for storing food. And many Old World monkeys have something else very special that New World monkeys don't — opposable thumbs just like yours.

Black-tailed marmoset
NEW WORLD

De Brazza's monkey
OLD WORLD

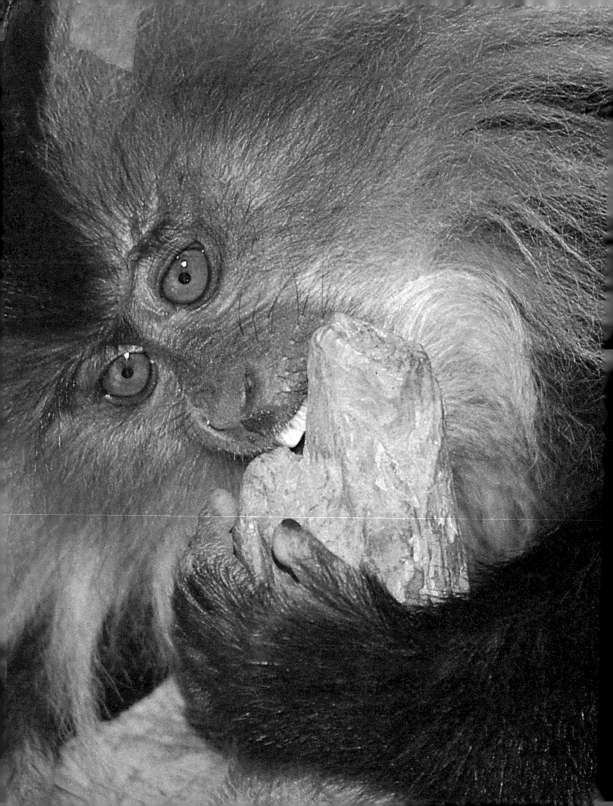

Thumbs Up

Take a close look at one of your hands and pick something up. Did you notice how you used your thumb and fingers together? Now try it again only this time without using your thumb. Not so easy, is it? We are able to move our thumb around to meet our fingers so we are said to have opposable thumbs.

Many Old World monkeys also have opposable thumbs. But they have something we don't have — opposable big toes! This means they can pick up objects as easily with their feet as they can with their hands. And these special toes and thumbs are very useful for climbing trees, swinging from branch to branch, peeling fruit and just about everything else.

Macaque hand

The hand of the lion-tailed macaque is very similar to your own, nails and all.

Real Troopers

Opposite page: *A troop of olive baboons on the move.*

Monkeys, like apes, lemurs and people, are primates. Old World monkeys are strong, agile animals with long limbs. In fact, their arms are about the same length as their legs, which helps them to be great climbers and also fast runners on all fours. Their tail varies from a mere stub to an elegant plume longer than their body. Their size ranges from the tiny talapoin, which weighs about a kilogram (2.2 pounds), to the mighty baboon, which may tip the scales at 45 kilograms (100 pounds).

Monkeys enjoy each other's company and rarely live alone. Some stay in pairs but most gather in groups known as troops. A troop may contain anywhere from 4 to over 100 individuals. Often one male plus several females and their young make up a troop.

High up in the trees monkeys have few enemies. While an occasional owl or hawk may attack a youngster, their main concern is other primates. However, those species that spend a lot of time on the ground have to be on the lookout for animals such as cheetahs, lions and jackals.

Monkey Sense

All monkeys are intelligent, but the Old World species are believed to be even brighter than their New World relatives. Apparently they rely less on instinct and more on reason. And they have an excellent memory, remembering from season to season where their favorite trees are and exactly when the fruit will be ripe.

Monkeys have very good eyesight and it's a good thing they do: leaping from branch to branch and being short-sighted could be quite a problem. Many mammals see the world in shades of gray, but monkeys see in color just as we do, and most of them see better in daylight than at night. Their sense of smell is good but not as keen as that of many other animals. They rely on their eyes more than their nose to find food. Since they have such small ears they often have to turn their head from side to side to zero in on sounds.

The Japanese macacque is known for its inventiveness as well as for its ability to withstand bitterly cold winters.

On the Menu

Many people think monkeys live mainly on bananas, but actually they eat an incredible variety of food. Here is a list of some of their favorite things: fruit, nuts, seeds, leaves, tubers, flowers, insects, spiders, crabs and birds' eggs. Some even eat small mammals. Many species live almost entirely on leaves. With their agile hands they have no trouble peeling fruit or removing bark from trees to find the juicy insects underneath. Of course monkeys also need water to live and most drink by drawing in water with their lips. A few, however, lap up water like a dog.

Monkeys must find fresh food each day since they store only what they can hold in their cheeks. Cheek pouches actually extend below the jaws and can pack quite a bit of food — possibly as much as a stomachful for some species.

One hand for food still leaves one for cuddling the baby. (Vervet monkeys)

Chitter Chatter

Monkeys talk to each other but not in words as we do. Instead they use a variety of different sounds, depending on whether they are happy, angry or afraid. Their most common call is a rapid chattering. When they are angry they shriek and scold each other. The loud call of the male rallies the rest of the troop together, warns of danger and lets other groups in the area know where he is and who's in charge.

Because monkeys have such expressive faces it is easy to tell what kind of mood they are in. Whether they are curious, content, happy or excited, you can see it on their faces. When it is angry a monkey pulls back its lips and shows its teeth. When it is tired or bored it lets out a big yawn.

*When a male hamadryas baboon shows his teeth, he **really** has something to show.*

Grooming Parties

Do you enjoy having your hair washed, dried and brushed? Many people find this relaxing. For monkeys, having their coat groomed is just as enjoyable, and it's helpful too. They spend a lot of time carefully removing dirt and insects from each other's hair, using their hands and often their teeth as well. Social standing in the troop determines who grooms who. Friends of equal status groom each other, while a male leader may have many lower ranking members wanting to groom him. Mothers and other females often groom the young ones.

Monkeys groom each other not only to rid themselves of pests, but often just for fun. In the same way that we like to visit with our friends, monkeys like to get together for a grooming party. It helps to calm them down and is probably a way of showing affection and friendship.

"Where on earth did you pick this up?" (Mandrills)

I'm All Ears

By the time most monkeys are four or five years old they are ready to start a family. Females mate with the leader of the troop to make sure they have the strongest, healthiest father for their offspring. Young males usually have to fight with older males for the chance to mate with females in the troop. Often it takes a male quite some time and many attempts at a number of troops before he wins a mate.

About six months after mating the female gives birth to a single infant — in rare cases twins. She usually has her baby at night high up in a tree. She does not make a nest or prepare any type of nursery. Immediately after birth the wide-eyed and alert youngster clings to the fur on its mother's belly. If it cannot support its own weight the mother will put her hand on its back for extra support. She also gives her baby its first bath by licking it clean.

Except for being able to grab hold, a newborn monkey is totally helpless. It is covered in soft velvety fur which is often a different color than that of its parents.

Opposite page:
Like most baby monkeys, this young hamadryas baboon has ears that seem way too big for its head.

Monkey See, Monkey Do

For the first few days of its life the newborn monkey spends its time sleeping and nursing on its mother's milk. It will be at least six months to a year before it will be weaned. In at least one species the baby monkey sucks its thumb.

In some families the father helps to look after his offspring and may even carry it around. Sometimes other members of the troop babysit the youngster. But no matter who is helping out, the mother keeps a watchful eye and ear out for her baby and will return to its side at the least sign of trouble.

By the third month the young monkey's coat is gradually replaced by a new fluffier one which is similar to its parents' fur but not as clearly marked. By this time too, the youngster has begun to learn by copying what its mother does. When mother and child go off looking for food, the young monkey eats the same things it sees her eating. Soon it knows what's good to eat and what isn't.

This baby silvered langur's spectacular orange coat will last only a few months.

Monkeying Around

Young monkeys are very active and love to play.
They chase each other, wrestle and scamper up
and down trees. Two of their favorite games are
follow the leader and king of the castle.
Sometimes they even tease their mother by
swinging on her tail! Luckily for them adult
monkeys are usually very patient and will put up
with a lot of "monkey business." Playing is not
only fun but it helps to make them good climbers
and teaches them to get along with others, which
is very important in a monkey troop.

Monkeys mature more slowly than other
animals their size. The bond between mothers
and daughters lasts into adulthood, and females
often stay in the troop they were born into.
Males, on the other hand, often leave and join
other young males in a temporary bachelor
group while they wait till they are able to join a
new troop.

Caught in the act!

Colorful Coats

In Africa the most common monkeys are the guenons. Most of them live high up in trees, seldom coming down to the ground. The main exceptions are the different types of green monkeys, who nest and take refuge in trees but spend most of their time on the ground.

All guenons have tails longer than their bodies and cheek pouches in which they store food they don't want to eat right away. Guenons are very handsome monkeys about the size of a housecat. Many have brightly colored coats with bold, contrasting patterns. Mustaches, beards and striped sideburns are also common, especially in the males. Their names — red-eared, owl-faced, white-nosed — give you some idea of what they look like. Guenons are quite tolerant of each other and in some areas several different species live happily side by side.

De Brazza's monkey.

Lanky Langurs

Lanky, lean, graceful, these are a few words that describe the langur monkeys of India and parts of the Far East. There are more than 50 different kinds and they come in a variety of sizes, shapes and colors. Some live in forests while others brave the chilly slopes of the Himalaya mountains. They are primarily leaf-eaters and have a special digestive system similar to that of a cow which helps them get as much nourishment as possible from their food.

Most langurs spend the majority of their time in trees. However, the gray or Hanuman langur is mainly a ground dweller. This langur is considered sacred in parts of India and is protected by law, free to roam the countryside and even city streets as it pleases. It is an adaptable monkey that lives in woodlands, forests and farmlands.

The handsome Hanuman.

Super Snout

Meet the Pinocchio of the monkey world, the proboscis monkey. The word proboscis means "long flexible snout" so it's no mystery how this comical-looking monkey got its name. Both the males and the females have long noses but the male's is sometimes so long it hangs below his chin. And the bigger the male's nose is, the more attractive females find him. This super snout is not just there for looks, however; it serves as a loudspeaker when the male gives his loud *honk-keehonk* warning call.

The proboscis monkey is found in swampy forests on the island of Borneo. Leaves make up the bulk of its diet and it spends a good part of the day resting between meals. It can be surprisingly active when it wants to, though. Despite its large size — up to 23 kilograms (52 pounds) for a male — it is an excellent climber. It is also a daring high diver and often jumps from trees into water over 15 metres (50 feet) below — and then dogpaddles away with ease. The proboscis monkey has a nose for trouble and when threatened will dive and swim underwater.

Opposite page:
Rather surprisingly, the super-sized nose of the proboscis monkey does not seem to give it a better sense of smell than other monkeys have.

Mangabey Monkeys

Mangabey monkeys live mainly in the forests of West and Central Africa. They come in a variety of colors but all have white upper eyelids that can been seen from great distances. They are slender, long-tailed animals weighing from 3 to 12 kilograms (7 to 26 pounds).

The deep grunting call of the gray-cheeked mangabey sounds like a "hesitant turkey with a frog in its throat." It is a rather noisy monkey that can often be heard high in treetops ripping a meal of bark from trees. It also eats fruit, flowers, insects and birds' eggs, and will bite the head off a snake before eating the rest of it. Gray-cheeked mangabeys have a larger home range than most forest monkeys because they are so effective at finding all available food in an area that they must wait quite a while before returning to it.

You probably won't be a bit surprised to learn that this mangabey monkey is commonly known as the red-capped mangabey.

Royal Family

Most people are familiar with the baboon, the largest of all monkeys. Males can grow to be over a metre (3 feet) tall. Females are about half that size. Baboons are known as dog-faced monkeys. Come to think of it, they do look a bit like a large poodle with their long muzzle. One species, the hamadryas baboon of Ethiopia and Arabia, is the famous sacred monkey of ancient Egypt that was often made into a mummy.

Baboons are ground dwellers and rarely climb trees except to sleep. Troops average about 40 individuals and travel 3 to 4 kilometres (2 to 2.5 miles) a day searching for food. It is believed that some baboons never move more than a metre (3 feet) away from another baboon in their entire life. Now that's togetherness!

Baboons have a reputation for being aggressive and when threatened they can indeed be very ferocious. Male baboons will fight a leopard or even a lion that threatens the troop. However, they are generally friendly and gentle with each other.

Opposite page:
While the hamadryas baboon can look quite imposing, it is actually the smallest of the baboons.

Big Bold and Beautiful

Opposite page:
We still know relatively little about how mandrills live in the wild.

Let's face it, animals don't get much more colorful than this. With its brilliant blue-ribbed cheeks, red nose and rosy bottom, the mandrill is one of a kind. The males have the brightest colors and when they get angry their face gets even more vivid. Females are not so gaudy and less than half the size of their mates.

Mandrills live in the forests of West Africa and for this reason are known as forest baboons. This is one animal you would not want to "monkey around" with. An adult male is as strong as a leopard and when threatened as powerful as a gorilla. Not to mention the fact that its canine teeth are as long as a tiger's.

Mandrills are big, measuring in at just under a metre (3 feet) tall. Their tails are short for a monkey, usually less than 10 centimetres (4 inches) long. Mandrills walk on their fingers and toes, never letting their palms touch the ground. To rest they often lean forward on their hands. They will eat almost anything, and when water is scarce they dig in the bottom of dry riverbeds to find it.

Fleet of Foot

If all the primates in the world were to have a race, no one would be able to keep up with the patas monkey. This streamlined, long-legged animal is built like a greyhound. With its bounding gait it can reach speeds of up to 55 kilometres (34 miles) an hour. The patas monkey lives in the savannah regions of Africa. Although it is a ground dweller it will often climb a small tree to find food or to take a quick look around. It also sleeps in trees at night.

The patas monkey belongs to the same family as do the guenons. With its reddish coat and its white mustache, it is a rather dashing looking monkey. Males weigh an average of 10 kilograms (22 pounds) although some may be twice that. Females are smaller, weighing in at about 7 kilograms (15 pounds) or less. A typical troop contains 20 animals or so. Patas monkeys are relatively quiet. Even when threatened they only make soft chirping sounds.

The patas monkey is also known as the hussar or military monkey.

Aerial Acrobats

Opposite page:
Black and white colobus monkeys actually begin life with a snow-white fur coat. The black fur starts growing in when they are about four months old.

The colobus monkey has a beautiful coat of long, fine hair. While there are red and olive colobuses, most are a striking black and white.

Colobus monkeys are known as leaf monkeys because they can eat large amounts of foliage. However, some species eat more fruit and seeds than they do leaves. They live in forests in the middle of Africa high up in the treetops. Incredible acrobats, they often leap 8 metres (25 feet) or more from branch to branch. They can even change direction in mid-air! But most of the time they move rather slowly, resting between feedings, and often travel only 500 metres (yards) in a day.

Colobus monkeys are unusual because they only have a small nub of a thumb or none at all. This is how they get their name, which means docked or mutilated. Having no thumbs doesn't slow down these monkeys, though. They are very skilled at picking up things and climbing trees with only their fingers and palms.

Feeling Frosty

There are more than 15 different species of macaque monkeys in the world. With the exception of one species they all live in Asia. Most have drab brown, gray or yellow coats but some have bright colored skin on their face. Macaques are essentially ground dwellers and are very good at walking on two feet.

Two well-known members of this family are the rhesus monkey, a favorite of zoos, and the Japanese macaque. The Japanese macaque lives the farthest north of all the monkeys in the world. During the winter when snow covers the forests and mountains of Japan and there are no leaves on the trees, these thick-coated animals survive by eating bark. They keep warm by huddling together and by taking dips in nearby hot springs where they dogpaddle in the steaming water.

Japanese macaque.

Helping Out

We owe a great deal to monkeys. Not only are they fascinating to watch, they have helped us in many ways. Thanks to well-trained monkeys many disabled people now have a much needed helper in the home. These faithful companions give their owners an independence never before possible.

Did you know the first astronaut was a rhesus monkey? And that's not its only claim to fame. Thanks to research with these monkeys a vaccine for polio was discovered and many children have been spared from this disabling disease. It was also by studying rhesus monkeys that scientists identified the Rh (for rhesus) positive and negative factors that exist in our blood as well as monkeys'. This too has saved many lives.

Monkeys certainly deserve our respect and protection. It is very important that we stop destroying their forests so that these amazing animals will always have a place to live.

Words to Know

Canine tooth   One of four strong pointed teeth, located between the front teeth and the molars.

Groom   To clean or brush, especially hair.

Home range   Area where an animal lives and looks for food.

Mate   To come together to produce young. Either member of an animal pair is also the other's mate.

Opposable thumb   The kind of thumb that is separated from the fingers and can be moved around to meet them. Humans and a few animals, including Old World monkeys and chimpanzees, have opposable thumbs.

Prehensile   Adapted for grabbing and holding, especially by wrapping around an object. Many New World monkeys and some other animals, such as opossums, have prehensile tails. Old World monkeys however do not.

Primate   An animal that belongs to the order Primates, such as a monkey, chimpanzee or human being.

Proboscis   A long, flexible snout (pronounced pro.BOSS.is).

Troop   A group of monkeys that live together with the strongest male in charge.

INDEX

Cover Photo: Bill Ivy
Photo Credits: Bill Ivy, pages 4, 8, 12, 16, 20, 28, 36, 39; George Holton, page 11; Robert Winslow, page 15; Nancy Adams, pages 19, 32, 35, 40; Fletcher & Baylis (Photo Researchers, Inc.), page 22; Brian Vikander (West Light), pages 24, 25; Nancy Staley, page 27; Fred Bavendam (Peter Arnold, Inc.), page 31; Gregory Dimijian (Photo Researchers, Inc.), page 43; Akira Uchiyama (Photo Researchers, Inc.), page 45.